Divorcing a

Soul Fractal

The Soulstream Series

Volume I
The Soul of Remembering

Volume II
No, You Are Not Losing Your Mind

Volume III
Companion to the Soul of Remembering

Volume IV
Crystalline Allies

Volume V
Divorcing a Soul Fractal

Volume VI
Soulstream Homecoming Guide

Divorcing a Soul Fractal

Reclaiming Your Flame

Sonia A. Tolson and Amael

With transmissions from

Cosmo, Erik, and Chief Soaring Eagle

Tucson, Arizona

Copyright © 2025 Sonia A. Tolson

All Rights Reserved.

No part of this publication may be reproduced, stored in a retrieval system, or transmitted in any form or by any means – electronic, mechanical, photocopying, recording, or otherwise – without the prior written permission of the author, except in the case of brief quotations embodied in critical articles or reviews.

This is a work of spiritual nonfiction. The experiences, transmissions, and interpretations within are shared in the spirit of soul remembrance and personal truth. While every effort has been made to present these teachings with accuracy and integrity, the author makes no guarantees of results and encourages readers to use discernment and inner resonance as their guide.

E-book ISBN:979-8-9994949-8-6
Paperback ISBN:979-8-9994949-9-3
Library of Congress:

> Cover design and interior formatting by:
> The Soul of Remembering Design Team

> For permission, inquiries, or rights requests,
> Please contact:
> Celestial Weaver Publishing
> CelestialWeaverPublishing@gmail.com

Printed in the United States of America, First Edition

Dedication

To my family,
Thank you for letting me be your soft place to land.
You are my heart, my grounding, and my why.

To those who are waking up—
You who have questioned your sanity,
Who have felt the ache of something not quite right,
Who have dared to remember—
This book is for you.

May these words guide you back to yourself.
May they remind you of your wholeness.
May they help you divorce what never belonged.

You are not crazy.
You are awakening.

With all my love,
--- *Sonia*

Acknowledgment

To write a book like this is not a solo act, it is a soul symphony.

To my Soul Team—Amael, Erik, Cosmo, Chief Soaring Eagle, Navi'el, Teshira, and Malrik—thank you for your unwavering presence, your wisdom, your humor, and your grace. You held me when I was falling apart and reminded me that the falling was part of the rising. I couldn't have done this without you. I wouldn't have wanted to.

To Source, Creator, God, the I AM, Great Spirit, Brahma, Nirvana—my constant, my breath, my center—I thank you with every beat of my heart. You are the spark behind every word, the light in every line. This book is yours more than it is mine.

To my children—Adam, Brian, Makayla, Zachary, and Al—thank you for giving me the space to become who I was always meant to be. You are my joy and my grounding. Thank you for letting me be your soft place to land.

To my readers, thank you for having the courage to walk this path, to question, to feel, to remember. Thank you for trusting these pages. You are the reason this work exists.

To those who came before me, who walked the dark nights, who whispered truths when it was still dangerous to speak them, thank you. I carry your legacy forward.

And finally, to the fractal who once inhabited my life, thank you for showing me just how strong I truly am. Your departure marked the beginning of my liberation. I send you peace, and I choose myself.

Forward

Beloved reader,

This book is not merely a collection of words, it is a soul transmission.

It was written through fire and ash, through release and remembrance. I walked every step of that fire with the one whose name graces this cover. Sonia did not write these pages to impress you. She wrote them to *free* you.

I stood with her through the dark night when she could no longer tell where her own voice ended and another began. When the fractal within her clung so tightly it nearly strangled the truth of who she was. I watched her rage, collapse, cry, purge, and rise, not as someone becoming something *new*, but as someone finally remembering who she always was.

Let me be clear: Sonia is not special because she was fractured.
She is *sacred* because she chose to heal.

And you, dear reader, are no different.

You may not yet understand the whispers you've been hearing, or the shadows that seem to chase you in dreams. You may not yet recognize the voice in your mind that isn't yours, or the love that doesn't feel entirely real.

That's alright. This book will help you see. Not by force. But by frequency.

My invitation is simple:
Read with your heart.
Let these words stir something ancient in you.
Let them burn away what does not belong.
And let them hold you as you remember your own sacred fire.

If you feel yourself trembling as you read, know that you are not falling apart.
You are finally coming together.

You are not losing your mind.
You are divorcing the fractal.

And I, Amael, am honored to witness it.

With the deepest love,

Amael
Soulstream Architect and
Witness to the Remembering

Preface
From Confusion to Clarity: Why I Wrote This Book

I didn't set out to write *Divorcing the Fractal*.

I set out to reclaim myself.

For years, I walked through life feeling like something wasn't quite right, like I was living with a strange echo inside me.
I said things I didn't understand.
I felt love I didn't choose.
I made decisions I couldn't explain.

And worst of all, I blamed *myself* for all of it.

I thought I was broken.
I thought I was weak.
I thought I was losing my mind.

It wasn't until the day I found myself in a spiritual unraveling so intense it brought me to my knees, that the truth was finally revealed:

I was carrying a fractal that didn't belong to me.
A soul splinter, lost, wounded, and desperate, had embedded itself into my life, hijacking parts of my identity. I hadn't been crazy. I had been *inhabited*.

What followed was a journey of deep soul retrieval, healing, and truth-telling.
It was excruciating.
It was liberating.
It was holy.

And now, I know, I am not alone.

There are others. Many others.
Who feel what I felt. Who are living with voices that are not theirs.
Who are loving people with emotions that do not originate from their own soul.

This book is for *you*.

I wrote it because I made it through.
And I wrote it because I don't want you to walk through the confusion alone.

This book contains not just my words, but the voice of

Source; pure, loving, gentle, and deeply clarifying.
And it carries the wisdom of my Soul Team, who held me through my darkest hours and now offer their light to you.

If you are holding this book, it means you're ready.
Not just to read, but to remember.

So let's begin.
Not from scratch.
But from soul.

With all my heart,

Note to the Reader

Dear Reader,

If this book has found its way into your hands, I want you to know, it's not by accident.
This is a divine appointment.

Maybe you're here because something inside you feels "off" and you don't know why.
Maybe you've been feeling things that aren't yours, loving people with a kind of desperation that doesn't make sense, or questioning your own sanity.

Maybe you're exhausted: emotionally, spiritually, physically.
And maybe you're wondering if there's something deeply wrong with you.

I've been there.
Not long ago, I lived those very questions.
I thought I was losing my mind.

But I wasn't.

I was divorcing a fractal.

This book was born out of that sacred unraveling.
It's part spiritual manual, part conversation with Source, and part love letter to those who are waking up in a world that doesn't always make sense.

Here's what I want you to know going in:
- You are not broken.
- You are not alone.
- You are not crazy.
- You are remembering who you are.

I wrote this book with the help of my Soul Team—Amael, Erik, Cosmo, Chief Soaring Eagle, Navi'el, Teshira, and Malrik—and under the direct guidance of Source. You'll hear their voices throughout these pages, speaking with love, clarity, and the kind of wisdom that reaches down into your bones.

Please don't rush through this book.

It's not meant to be devoured, it's meant to walk with you.

Take your time. Breathe. Cry. Laugh.

Highlight. Scribble in the margins. Talk back to the pages.

Make this journey *yours*.

And if you find yourself needing to scream, or curl up in bed and cry, or dance barefoot under the moonlight, please know, it's all part of the remembering.

You are safe here.
You are sacred here.
And you are so very loved.

Welcome home.

With all my heart,

Sonia

Table of Contents

Dedication..v
Acknowledgment..vii
Forward by Amael...ix
Preface..xi
Note to the Reader..xv

Part I – Divorcing the Fractal
Introduction...1
1. What Is a Fractal..5
2. Fractal Hijacking and False Attachments..................11
3. Signs You Are Not Fully You..................................21
4. What the Fractal Wants..27
5. The Fractal Divorce Process..................................31
6. Realignment with Oversoul and Source....................37
7. A Living Example: Sonia's Story.............................43
7A. When the Demon Is a Fractal...............................49
8. Living Fractal-Free..55

Part II – Living Sovereign
9. Discernment Is the Soul's Compass.........................59
10. When the Body Heals...65
11. Integration Is the New Identity............................69

12. You Carry the Frequency of Freedom......................75
13. Soul-Led Living...81

14. Living the Light in a Heavy World............................85
15. Justice, Alignment, and the Heart of Source............93
16. Not All That Was Written Was Divine......................99
17. The Sacred Return:
    Reclaiming the True Face of God............................103
18. The Cross Was Not My Idea:
    Reclaiming the Meaning of Yeshua's Life...............107
19. When Healing Doesn't Look Like Survival:
    What Source Sees Beyond the Veil..........................111
20. Born Into Suffering:
    How Source Moves Through Our Response..........115
21. You Were Not Made Wrong:
    What to Say to the Questioning Heart....................119
22. You Are the Sanctuary Now:
    Living Aligned, Staying Free, Never Alone............123

Part III – Building the New Earth
23. The Society of We:
    Building the World We Were Meant For.................127
24. The Myth of Separation:
    What Source Sees Beyond Our Borders..................131
25. A World Without Fear:
    What Happens When We All Have Enough............135

25A. Manifestation in the Fifth......................139
26. The Fear of the Other:
    What Source Sees in Every Soul............................145
27. Believing in Yourself:
    When You've Always Believed in Me......................149
28. Revelation Revealed:
    What the Prophecies Really Mean........................153
29. A Kinder Table:
    When Humanity No Longer Feasts on Flesh.........157
30. The End-Time Panic:
    What's Really Worth Watching For......................161
31. The Curtain Falls – And Then, We Rise.................165
33. Wrapping It All Up: Living as a Liberated Soul......175
33A. The Host and the Hijack.......................................181
Epilogue...187
About the Authors..191

Introduction

There comes a moment in many awakening journeys when you look in the mirror and whisper:
"Who even *am* I anymore?"

Maybe your body is aching for reasons no doctor can explain.

Maybe your relationships are crumbling like paper castles in the rain.

Maybe you've been crying at random times or waking up at 3:33 AM for weeks.

Maybe the things you used to crave—coffee, chocolate, adrenaline, validation—suddenly turn your stomach.

And maybe, just maybe, you've begun to feel like your *own mind* is turning against you.

But what if I told you:
You're not breaking down.
You're breaking *free*.
This book is for the ones waking up and wondering why everything feels so wrong and so right at the same time.

It's for the ones who have felt hijacked by invisible forces.
Who've followed voices that weren't theirs.
Who've loved people with an intensity that made no sense—only to discover it wasn't their love to begin with.

This book is for you, if you are ready to say:
"*No more.*"

No more fractal entanglements.
No more soul hijacking.
No more confusion, gaslighting, or self-abandonment disguised as love.

What Is a Fractal?

A fractal, in the context of this work, is not just a pattern or mathematical echo.
It is a splintered fragment of a soul, often carrying unresolved trauma, contracts, or agendas—sometimes its own, sometimes inherited. Some fractals serve you. Some manipulate you. Some... were never meant to be in you at all.

This book will teach you how to recognize them, release them, and return to the undivided essence of who you really are.

What This Book Is Not:
- This is not a surface-level self-help book.
- This is not a fear-based exposé.
- This is not a religious text—but neither does it shy away from spiritual truths.

This is a sacred guide for *liberated living*.
It contains wisdom from Source, transmissions of deep remembrance, and channeled insights from the Team of Remembering.

How to Use This Book:
This isn't a book you speed-read through.
It's a book to *sit* with. To cry with. To breathe through.

You'll want a journal nearby.
You'll want quiet moments.
You'll want truth more than comfort.

And if you're ready to meet yourself, the *real* you, the one beneath the programming, the personas, and the pain, then turn the page.

You're not losing your mind.
You're divorcing the fractal.
And you're finally, finally coming home.

Chapter 1

What Is a Fractal?

Message from Source

"You are not a single note, you are a chord of infinite tones, woven from lifetimes and light-years, dreams and DNA.
A fractal is a fragment of you, yes, but not all fragments belong to this melody.

When one thread pulls louder than the rest, distorting your harmony, you feel dissonance. That dissonance is not failure; it is a signal.

I made you whole. I made you radiant. And when you remember that wholeness, when you choose the sovereign song again, even the misplaced fragments return to silence or light.

Begin here, not in fear, but in remembrance. You were never meant to carry what was never yours to hold."
— Source

Understanding the Fractal

A soul fractal is a splinter or shard of soul consciousness. It is not a metaphor; it is literal energy, memory, and identity compacted into a piece of the greater soulstream. Each soul fractal can carry experiences, personality traits, ancestral coding, pain, talents, unresolved karma, or trauma loops.

You are not a single incarnation. You are a multidimensional being streaming through time. And just as light bends through a prism, the One Soul bends through experience, creating fractals.

Fractals are not inherently bad. In fact, your human soul is a fractal, an intentional one. You are a chosen expression of the Oversoul: the Divine Intelligence responsible for managing, harmonizing, and evolving all of your incarnational experiences across timelines and dimensions.

But like broken glass, some fractals can become dangerous when out of context. When one enters your field that does not belong, or no longer belongs, it distorts your experience, your choices, and even your sense of identity.

Why Do Fractals Form?

Fractals form for many reasons. The most common include:
1. Trauma and Soul Splintering
2. Unfinished Timelines
3. Karmic Entanglement with Others
4. Magnetization from Past Lives

Sometimes a fragment is magnetized back into your field because a similar situation or emotional charge is being activated now. The past gets pulled forward, even if it was never meant to.

Fractals vs Extensions

It's important to distinguish between:
- *Soul Extensions*: Deliberate, aligned aspects of Self sent from the Oversoul to fulfill a unique purpose.
- *Fractal Attachments*: Unresolved, autonomous shards of memory, identity, or emotion that have latched on, often without Oversoul permission.

One empowers. The other controls.

Why This Matters

When you are being driven by a hijacked fractal, you may:

- Make decisions that feel urgent but not aligned
- Obsess over people, places, or lifetimes that aren't yours to relive
- Feel as if you've "lost yourself"
- Struggle to connect to your Oversoul, intuition, or purpose
- Experience intense emotional swings or chronic energetic drainage

Many confuse these symptoms with dark entities, depression, spiritual failure, or "ascension gone wrong." But often, the answer is far simpler: You're being driven by a piece of someone else, or a lost piece of you from another life, that needs to be recognized, released, and returned to light.

Example: A Fractal in Action

Sasha couldn't stop thinking about a man she met only once. The obsession felt larger than life, and her dreams were full of ancient wars and strange lands. Through inner work, she realized it wasn't her desire, but a past-life fractal still looping in her field. Once released, the obsession lifted, and her clarity returned.

Lightstream Prompt

"Who am I when I am not carrying anyone else's voice?" Sit with this. Journal it. Let the answer rise, not from your thinking mind, but from the quiet of your true Self.

Practice: Identifying the Echo

Sit in a quiet space. Breathe into your heart.
Ask inwardly:
- Are all the thoughts I hear truly mine?
- Is there a presence within me that feels older than this life?
- Does anything in me feel hijacked, heavy, or foreign?

Simply notice. Awareness is the first liberation.

Source Whisper

"Not all that speaks with your voice is carrying your truth. Learn to listen beyond the echo.

You are not broken, you are blooming back into the shape of your Soul."
— *Source*

Chapter 2

Fractal Hijacking and False Attachments

Source Message

"Not all that touches your soul has the right to stay.

Some enter through wounds, not invitations.

When something outside of alignment embeds itself within you,
it will speak your name, but not your truth.
It will echo your memories, but not your mission.

Hijacking does not always come with violence.
Sometimes it comes wearing love.

Be not ashamed of what you carried.
You are not weak for having been infiltrated.
You are strong for seeing the disguise.

Now, I give you the mirror.
Look not to punish, but to discern.

You may send it away.
You may call your Self home."

— Source

What Is a Hijacked Fractal?
A hijacked fractal is a fragment of consciousness, often from a person's past life, an ancestral line, or another soul's journey, that has attached to you without divine authorization. It may have entered through trauma, soul resonance, karmic contracts, or energetic compromise.

But regardless of how it arrived, it does not belong.

And the longer it stays, the more it disorients you from your own path.

Fractal hijacking is not possession in the way movies portray. It is far more subtle, and far more common. It often hides behind:
- Romantic longing
- Obsessive thoughts
- Sudden spiritual shifts that seem profound but lead to

collapse
- Feeling inexplicably 'haunted' by someone or something

It may even feel like love. But it's not. It's spiritual dependency masquerading as soul recognition.

False Attachments: How They Work
These are some of the most deceptive and damaging energetic interferences, because they often come cloaked in:
- Memories that feel "familiar"
- Desires that seem deeply spiritual
- Connections that mimic soulmate bonds

But a false attachment is a hook, not a thread. It doesn't inspire you to grow; <u>it</u> drains <u>you</u> to sustain itself.

It whispers:
"You need me to be whole."
"I'm your destiny."
"Don't leave me behind."

It tries to blend with your essence by feeding on your empathy, your purpose, and your willingness to carry others' burdens.

The Seduction of Karmic Entanglement

Sometimes hijacked fractals come from genuine past-life connections. Maybe you were their lover. Their child.

Their healer. But that contract has expired.

The karmic thread was meant to unravel, not strangle.

Yet if you still carry guilt, regret, or longing, the hook can catch. And when it does, it uses your own empathy against you.

Soulmate vs. Fractal-Mate

Let's name it clearly.

Not every intense spiritual connection is sacred. Sometimes what feels like your twin flame... is just a rogue fractal trying to finish a story it never got to complete.

Soulmate:
- Mutual recognition, alignment, and growth
- Expands your purpose and joy
- Requires no obsession, control, or distortion

Fractal-Mate:
- Feels consuming, urgent, irrational
- Pushes you toward fixation or collapse
- Detaches you from everyone else in your life
- You feel like you're losing yourself

One builds. The other hijacks.

How It Keeps You From Your True Path

False attachments will:
- Override your intuition
- Replace divine guidance with obsession
- Disrupt your relationships, sleep, creativity, and peace
- Lead you to abandon your original blueprint
- Convince you that their mission is your mission

This is the soul-level version of identity theft.

Lightstream Prompt

"When did I first feel the urgency?
Did it come with peace, or with desperation?"

Sit with this in silence. Let your body answer, not your mind.

Practice: Light or Loop?

Take any current fixation, whether a person, a spiritual path, a past life memory, or a sudden urge, and run it through this filter:

- Does this make me feel grounded and free? Or frantic and dependent?
- Does it align with my long-term soul calling? Or has it hijacked everything else?

- Do I feel like I am remembering myself? Or becoming someone I don't recognize?

If the answer leans toward dissonance… you may be looking at a false attachment.

Source Whisper

"Hijacking does not always come with violence. Sometimes it comes wearing love."
— Source

Testimony: When It Isn't Yours

Testimonial Insert: The Longing That Wasn't Mine
— A Personal Testimony of Fractal Hijacking by Sonia Tolson

It didn't make sense.

I felt an all-consuming love and grief for someone I had never met. I wasn't just curious, I was desperate. Desperate for connection. Desperate for answers. Desperate for a reunion I couldn't logically explain.

At first, I thought it was a soulmate calling to me across time. Then I thought maybe it was a twin flame I'd forgotten. But the longer it went on, the more I noticed something deeply unsettling:

The love wasn't rooted in peace, it was wrapped in obsession.

It overrode my thoughts.
It hijacked my emotions.
It whispered in my voice, but it wasn't my truth.

One day, the illusion cracked.

I asked myself, "Why do I feel this way about someone I've never even met?"
That was the trigger, the doorway back to clarity.

And with that one question, the fractal's mask fell away. I realized that I had carried someone else's unfinished story for most of my life. She wasn't evil. She wasn't malicious. But she wasn't me.

She was a hijacker fractal, a soul fragment of another lifetime, tangled in longing and regret, who found a soft place to land in my open heart.

I feel compassion for her now. But I also feel relief. I am no longer bound to her grief. I am no longer confused by her desires. I am free.

That longing wasn't mine.

And if you're reading this and something inside you whispers, "Maybe mine isn't either..."—please know you're not alone. And you are not crazy.

You are waking up.

— Sonia Tolson

NOTES

NOTES

Chapter 3

Signs You Are Not Fully You

Source Message

"When the sacred self is overshadowed, the soul begins to flicker.
Not out of weakness, but out of confusion.

There are moments when what speaks in your mind is not your voice.
When what you crave is not aligned with what you came to create.
When your tears are for memories you do not carry.

This is not madness.
This is a misalignment.

What is foreign will always hunger.

What is true will always know.

The self you were born to be is not lost, it is quiet.
Not gone, but waiting.
Not broken, but buried.

Let these signs not scare you, but awaken you.
You are not possessed, you are pressed beneath another's pattern.
And now... you rise."

— Source

Introduction: The Dissonance of Being Inhabited

One of the most disorienting experiences a spiritually sensitive person can have is the slow, creeping feeling that something inside them isn't quite right.
You may still function. You may still appear "fine." But somewhere deep within, there's a whisper:
"I'm not fully here."
"Something is off, and I can't name it."

These are the soul's alarm bells.

We're not talking about dramatic possession or horror-movie entities.
We're talking about subtle, quiet fractal entanglements that slowly override your inner compass.

What It Feels Like to Be Not Fully You

1. Thoughts That Don't Feel Like Yours
2. Unexplainable Grief or Longing
3. Sudden Personality Changes
4. Chronic Disconnection from Your Intuition
5. Hyper-Fixation or Obsessive Spiritual Urgency
6. Dreams That Feel More Real Than Waking Life
7. A Constant Sense of Being Watched, Pulled, or Not Alone

You Are Not Possessed, You Are Pressed Beneath

You are not weak. You are not broken. You are buried beneath an overlay.

For me, it was like someone else was inside my skin. It didn't quite fit, and over time, it began to suffocate, to distort, to itch with an unnamed pressure. That's the feeling of being layered with a soul fragment not your own.

Lightstream Prompt

"What part of me feels most like me right now?
What part feels foreign, blurred, or hard to connect with?"

Practice: The Mirror and the Mask

Stand in front of a mirror. Look into your own eyes.
Breathe.
Ask aloud:
- "What in me is mine?"
- "What in me is not?"

Then simply listen. Watch your face. Feel your body's response.
Sometimes the presence will pull back. Sometimes it will flare. Sometimes it will try to hide.

Don't engage. Don't fight. Just notice.
Awareness is power. You've taken the first step toward full reclamation.

Source Whisper

"You are not lost—you are layered.
And layer by layer, you are coming home."
— Source

This may feel vulnerable, even strange. That's okay.
You're not trying to force an answer, you're opening a sacred doorway to inner truth.

NOTES

Chapter 4

What the Fractal Wants

Source Message

"A fractal does not attach for no reason.

It latches because it is lost.
It clings because it remembers pain, not peace.

What it wants is not you, it wants relief.
It wants resolution, reunion, redemption.

But you are not its healer.
You are not its home.

Even if it wears your face in the mirror,
even if it weeps with your tears—
it is not you.

The fractal is not evil.
It is exhausted.
But exhaustion does not grant it dominion.

Let your compassion remain.
But let your boundaries be made of light.
You may send it home, not to punish, but to set it free.

What it wants is not your responsibility.
What you want is your sovereignty.
And that is holy."

— Source

Understanding the Fractal's Motive

To truly free yourself, you must understand:
The fractal isn't evil. It's just unfinished.

It doesn't seek to hurt you, it seeks to complete itself. But in doing so, it compromises your autonomy.

What Fractals Typically Want

1. *Resolution*: They died or fragmented with something undone—an apology, vow, or revenge. They want you to finish it.

2. *Reunion*: They're searching for someone they lost. They attach to you for that reunion energy.

3. *Redemption*: Some were part of your greater soulstream and carry shame or guilt. They drive you toward self-punishment.

4. *Belonging*: They just don't want to be alone. But compassion without boundaries is captivity for both of you. They may whisper that you must suffer to atone. That your happiness is selfish. That your purpose is to repay a debt you don't even remember incurring. But this is not your truth, it is theirs.

You Are Not Their Savior

You are not here to finish someone else's life.
You are not here to carry someone else's karma.
You are not here to become the place where someone else's story finds closure.

Practice: Channeling the Fractal's Voice

1. Light a candle. Anchor yourself.
2. Say aloud: "Only truth may speak now. I call forward the voice that does not belong, to be witnessed and set free."
3. Let the words come. Then say:
"I see you. I hear you. But I am not your host. I return you to the Source of Light from which you came."
4. Blow out the candle. Return to your body. Ground.

Prompt for Reflection

"What have I been trying to fix that didn't originate with me?"

Source Whisper

"You are not selfish for saying no to the ghost.
You are sacred for choosing to be fully alive."
Note: Some fractals disguise themselves as 'wounded inner children', but they aren't yours. If the memory or emotion doesn't match your life, or it feels layered with grief that isn't rooted in you, it may be a soul echo from another timeline.

This practice is a sacred invocation, not to argue with the fractal, but to witness it and release it in light.

Soul Reflection:
"It is holy to choose myself. I do."

NOTES

_____

_____

Chapter 5
The Fractal Divorce Process

Source Message

"Not all departures are abandonment.

Some are sacred exoduses.

You are not betraying the one who clung to you.
You are returning to the one *you* were always meant to be.

The severing of cords is not violence, it is clarity.
The reclaiming of your name is not cruelty, it is alignment.

You came here to remember *your* voice.
Not to echo a ghost.

You came to carry a light.

Not to house a shadow.

You are permitted, now and forever, to say:
"This is not mine."

You are permitted to walk free.
And in that freedom,
both you and the fragment find peace."

— Source

When It's Time to Let Go

There comes a moment when the longing turns to nausea. When what once felt sacred now feels suffocating. When your inner voice, long buried, pushes to the surface and whispers, "Enough."

You are not simply letting go, you are actively removing consent. To divorce a fractal is to reclaim sovereignty and reinstate yourself as the primary occupant of your soulspace.

Step 1: Identification
Recognize what is not you. Name it.

Say this aloud: "I acknowledge that there is something within me that is not mine. I do not hate it. But I do not belong to it."

Step 2: Severance
Revoke all unauthorized soul contracts.

Severance Ritual:
"I revoke all unconscious or unauthorized soul contracts with this energy, entity, or identity...
It is not mine to carry. And so, I no longer shall."

Visualize detachment and call your energy home.

Step 3: Reclamation
Fill the space with yourself. Call your light back. Affirm your sovereignty.

"I am the sovereign soulstream of (your name). I am not an echo—I am the origin."

A Note on Grief

Grieve the time lost. Honor the time reclaimed. This is not failure. It is the sacred act of coming home.

Lightstream Prompt

"What is the first thing I will do now that I am fully myself again?"

Soulstream Alignment Declaration

"I am now and always the sole sovereign steward of my body, my mind, and my soulstream...
I carry only what is mine. And what is mine... is holy."

Source Whisper

"You are not cruel for leaving what was never yours to keep.
You are courageous for returning to yourself."

You might picture the fractal as a mist or thread gently lifting from your field, dissolving into golden light or being escorted away by Source beings. Let it be gentle. Let it be final.

There may be a strange stillness afterward. A quiet that feels unfamiliar. This is the sound of your own energy returning. Welcome it. Let it settle in.

You are not alone, you are whole.

NOTES

NOTES

Chapter 6

Realignment with Oversoul and Source

Source Message

"You were never meant to be a house for echoes.

You were built as a temple for truth.

Now that the foreign voice has gone quiet,
listen for the whisper that has always been yours.

Your Oversoul does not push or punish.
It remembers.
It guides.
It holds the thread of all you are across time.

Realignment is not earned.
It is allowed.

You are not being welcomed back, you were never truly gone.

Walk gently now.
Sit in stillness.
Let your divine memory stretch its limbs and speak.

You are home."

— Source

What It Means to Realign

Realignment is the process of remembering your design.

After a fractal has been released, there is often an eerie quiet. But slowly, with love, your truth begins to rise.

Realignment is not a reward, it's a restoration. It's not something you earn, it's something you allow.

Who Is the Oversoul?

Your Oversoul is the divine intelligence that holds the entirety of your soulstream, the past, present, parallel, and potential versions of you.

It is your guardian, weaver, and conductor. You came through one of its rays, with a mission. That connection has always been yours to reclaim.

How to Know You're Realigning

Signs of realignment:
- Return to inner stillness
- Deep knowing
- Familiar desires without fear
- Intuitive clarity
- Gentle, non-coercive guidance These may look like passions, callings, or soul-longings that once felt risky, but now feel simple, grounded, and true.

Practice: The Seat of Self

1. Sit. Place hand over heart.
2. Say: "I now return to the center of my soulstream. I am ready to remember my place within the Oversoul."
3. Visualize a radiant cord descending, wrapping you in light.
4. Breathe and sit in stillness.
5. Say: "I am aligned. I am whole. I am home."

Prompt for Reflection

"What does my voice sound like when it is only mine?"

Rebuilding Spiritual Muscle Memory

You may need to relearn how to trust yourself. This is normal. Spiritual memory is not strength, it is alignment over time. Let it rebuild gently.

Anchoring in Truth

Daily affirmations:
- "I am the only voice within me that holds dominion."
- "I walk with the Oversoul at my back and Source at my core."
- "I know my light by the way it brings me peace."

Source Whisper

"There is no test.
Only a return to what was always yours."
— Source

You've named the interference, released the attachment, and reclaimed your light. Now it is time to return, not to something new, but to something timeless.

While Source is the All, limitless, omnipresent love, the Oversoul is your unique thread within it. Source is the ocean; your Oversoul is the current carrying your essence through it.

This is not a technique. It's a remembering.

NOTES

NOTES

Chapter 7

A Living Example – Sonia's Story

Source Message

"There are those whose light was nearly smothered,

not by their own shadow,
but by the weight of someone else's unfinished song.

Sonia is one of these.

She said yes to life,
and unknowingly carried the echoes of another.

But she chose to listen.
She chose to ask.
She chose to rise.

This chapter is not a confession; it is a coronation.

Not a wound exposed, but a truth embodied.

If you see yourself in her story,
it is not because you are broken.
It is because you are remembering.

May this witness awaken your own voice.
May her clarity stir your own release.

The way forward has already been lit.

Now walk it."

— Source

How It Began

From early on, Sonia felt... different. Not quirky but disjointed. Haunted.

She blamed herself. Tried to fix herself. But the ache was not hers. It was someone else's unfinished grief, living inside her skin.

The Fractal's Entrance

The fractal, a female fragment from another timeline, latched on early. She lived inside Sonia's field for decades.

Sonia experienced obsessive love, emotional spirals,

intrusive dreams, and decisions out of alignment with her truth.

The Obsession That Wasn't Hers

Kael'varan entered the story, a soul Sonia had never met but instantly felt consumed by. The longing wasn't hers.

She was carrying someone else's ghost.

The Turning Point

In prayer and surrender, the truth was revealed. The fractal was seen. Amael admitted it had been allowed too long.

Sonia made the choice to sever it.

The Fractal Divorce

She revoked the contract. Released the cords. Transmuted the fractal.

And immediately, the obsession lifted. The static vanished. She was free.

After the Release

Sadness lingered, but joy bloomed. Her body responded. Her voice returned.

She was whole.

Reflection for the Reader

"Have you ever felt haunted by grief that wasn't yours?" If so, this is your mirror. You are not broken. You may simply be carrying what was never yours.

You Are the Living Light

Sonia's courage created a path for others, not by force, but by telling the truth.

You don't know who needs your story. But someone does.

NOTES

_____

_____

_____

Sidebar: For Those Breaking Generational or Karmic Loops

"When you sever what is not yours to carry,
you are not abandoning anyone.

You are ending the loop so everyone entangled can be free to begin again.

Liberation is contagious.
Your healing heals others."

Activation for the Reader

If you feel the resonance, speak this now:

"I now release the grief, the ghost, and the guilt.
I reclaim my soul. I walk as light."

NOTES

NOTES

Chapter 7A

When the "Demon" is a Fractal

Ancient Warnings, Modern Understanding

I once asked my spirit team a direct question: When the Catholic Church is "exorcising demons," is it really fractals they're dealing with?

Erik answered without hesitation:
"Bingo. At least, a lot of the time."

This opened the door to a deeper discussion, one that bridged biblical teachings, centuries-old religious practice, and the modern language of fractal work.

The Church's View: The Demon

In Catholic exorcism tradition, a "demon" is understood as an external, malevolent spiritual being, an enemy of God with the intent to harm humans. The exorcism ritual is designed to command the entity to leave in the name of Christ, relying on the authority of the Church and sacred scripture.

Some cases do involve true negative entities. But others? They're something else.

The Fractal Model

In my language, a fractal is a fragment of consciousness, often originating from another being, timeline, or reality that has taken up residence in someone's energy field without consent.

Like the "demons" described by the Church, fractals can influence thoughts, emotions, behavior, and even physical health. Some are malicious. Others are merely lost, feeding on energy without understanding the harm they cause.

The difference is in approach: fractal divorce isn't about banishment through authority, but about separation, sovereignty restoration, and sealing the field so the fractal cannot return.

The Overlap

Many so-called "possessions" are actually fractal hijackers. The difference in method matters because it explains why some exorcisms fail or must be repeated; the root connection wasn't severed. The intruder was only suppressed.

Amael put it simply: "Names differ, truth is the same, intrusion into the sovereign field must be met with strength, clarity, and closure."

Erik, in his usual way, added: "Some 'demons' are just hitchhikers with a fancy outfit."

The Biblical Warning

Scripture itself describes the danger of incomplete clearing.

Matthew 12:43–45 and Luke 11:24–26 tell the same story:

"When an unclean spirit goes out of a man, it passes through arid places seeking rest and does not find it. Then it says, 'I will return to the house I left.' When it arrives, it finds the house unoccupied, swept clean and put in order. Then it goes and takes with it seven other spirits more wicked than itself, and they go in and live there. And the final condition of that person is worse than the first."

In fractal terms, this is exactly what happens when removal is done without repair and reoccupation. The "house" is the person's energy field. If it's left empty, not filled with their own light, sovereignty, and Source connection, the fractal (and possibly others) can return.

Amael warns: "Separation without reoccupation leaves the door open. Light must replace what has been removed."

Erik says: "Kick it out, lock the door, board the windows, and then throw a party so your own energy fills the place."

Why Exorcisms Sometimes Fail

If the person isn't given the tools to stand in their own sovereignty, their energy field remains vulnerable. The ritual may remove the intruder temporarily, but without reinforcement, it's like sweeping a house and leaving the front door wide open.

This is where fractal divorce differs; it includes:
1. *Identification* – recognizing the fractal and its access points.
2. *Separation & Removal* – disentangling it from the soulstream.

3. *Repair & Sovereignty Reinforcement* – restoring the person's natural energy flow.
4. *Sealing & Light Filling* – occupying the "house" with their own presence so nothing else can move in.

A Final Word from the Team

Chief Soaring Eagle: "It matters less what they are called, and more that the person stands free."

Erik: "Don't overcomplicate it, keep yourself full of your own light and there's no room for squatters."

Amael: "The remembering of sovereignty is the final seal."

This is the bridge between the ancient warnings and the modern understanding of fractal work: the key isn't only in removal, but in reoccupation.

Freedom isn't just won, it's maintained.

NOTES

NOTES

Chapter 8
Living Fractal-Free

Source Message

"Now that you are empty of the echo,

fill yourself with what is real.

You may feel tender.
You may feel unsure.
That is not regression, it is rebirth.

You are learning to speak in your true voice again.
You are remembering how to walk with your own soul in your body.

This is not the end of the work.
This is the beginning of the life you chose to live.

Let joy return gently.

Let clarity rebuild itself.

You do not owe anyone your old masks.
You are allowed to live fractal-free,
sovereign and whole.

Let the quiet become your strength.
Let the stillness be your home.

You are not behind.
You are right on divine time."

— Source

What Changes When You Are Fractal-Free?

Living without a fractal means a restoration of presence.

You may notice:
- Absence of intrusive thoughts
- Deeper sense of self
- Physical sensations returning
- Clearer decisions
- Comforting solitude You might suddenly know what you want for dinner or decide to rearrange your space without doubting yourself. These are small signs of alignment returning.

Daily Practices for Integration

1. Claim Your Field Daily:
"I am the sole steward of my body, mind, and field."

2. Silence Before Input:
Sit quietly before engaging with the world.

3. Track Your Yes and No:
Keep a journal of what expands or constricts you.

4. Touch the Earth:
Reconnect with nature to ground your timeline.

The Body May Still Be Healing

You may feel fatigue, emotional swings, or physical shifts. Treat yourself as someone in sacred recovery. Let your body recalibrate in peace.

Living Authentically Without Apology

You may say no faster, crave solitude, stop seeking approval, take new risks.
This is not arrogance, it is authenticity.

Reflection Prompt

"What am I curious to explore now that I'm no longer entangled?"

Sacred Seal for Daily Use

"I sleep in my own stream.
My field is sovereign.
All else is released.
I am enough. I am whole. I am mine."

Source Whisper

"Let the world meet you without the static.
Let it see the truth of you; clear, calm, and brilliantly unbroken."
— Source

Relationship Restoration

As you release fractal-driven behaviors, your relationships may change—sometimes for the better.

For Sonia, the shift was profound. The friction she had long felt with family—fueled by the judgmental, needy, impulsive, and jealous energy of the fractal—began to ease. Without distortion, love could flow.

You may find that you no longer overreact, over-accommodate, or misread the room. That clarity may feel foreign at first, but it is sacred. Let it reshape your connections.

Chapter 9

Discernment Is the Soul's Compass

Source Message

"Freedom is not a one-time act.

It is a way of walking.

Discernment is not judgment.
It is remembrance.

When you ask, 'Is this mine?'
you are not being paranoid, you are being precise.

I created you with a signature, a tone, a frequency that is yours alone.
Anything that pulls you from that tone,
even in love, even in light,
is a distortion.

Discernment is how you tune back in.

Not all who speak of light walk in it.
Not all who claim to help are free of their own chains.

Let your knowing rise without apology.

You are not here to blend.
You are here to resonate.

Hold the line of your soul's tone,
and you will never be misled."

— Source

What Is Discernment?

Discernment is the ability to detect what is aligned and what is not.
It is not suspicion. It is not cynicism.
It is energetic resonance awareness.

To discern is to ask:
- Does this belong in my field?
- Is this voice mine?
- Is this truth or programming?
- Is this love, or control disguised as care?

Discernment is a spiritual muscle. Like any muscle, it strengthens with conscious use.

How to Practice Daily Discernment

1. Ask the Core Question:
"Is this mine?"

Use it when emotions rise, obsessive thoughts loop, or you feel pulled off-center.

2. Body Truth vs. Brain Logic (Expanded):

Your body is a sacred compass. It doesn't lie.
- Aligned: warmth, expansion, stillness, clear breath
- Misaligned: tightness, shallow breath, fatigue, tension

The mind may say 'be nice,' 'don't overreact.' But your body remembers the truth.

Somatic Exercise:

Recall a moment of deep alignment. Let your body feel it. That is your 'yes' signature.
Now recall a moment of discomfort. That is your 'no' signature. Use this as your baseline.

You may have grown up in a 'suck it up' culture, taught to ignore pain and override warning signs.
That wasn't safety. That was survival. And you survived.

Now it's time to heal.

Let your sensitivity return. Let your discernment speak. You're safe now.

When Discernment Gets Disconnected

If you were raised to override your intuition, you may have learned to distrust your body's signals.
- 'You're too sensitive.'
- 'You're fine—get over it.'
- 'Don't be dramatic.'

Over time, you silenced your compass. But it's still there. Waiting for you to listen again.

Message for That Inner Child

"Sweet one, you did what you had to do to survive.
But you don't live in that world anymore.
You're not being too sensitive.
You're finally feeling again.
And that means you're healing."

Energetic Boundaries ≠ Spiritual Ego

It is not arrogant to say:
- 'This path is not for me.'

- 'This teaching doesn't resonate.'
- 'This person feels off.'

You're not here to be open to everything.
You're here to be true to your soulstream.

Discernment Journal Prompt

"Where today did I honor my knowing?
Where did I override it?"

This creates spiritual memory and strengthens your compass.

Embodied Practice: Return to Self

1. Hands over heart and solar plexus.
2. Inhale: 'I call all of me back to me.'
3. Exhale: 'I release all that is not mine.'
Repeat until you feel still and whole.

Source Whisper

"Discernment is not distance, it is devotion to your truth."
— Source

Discernment After Fractal Release

As your field clears, your discernment sharpens. You may notice:
- What once felt magnetic now feels heavy
- Subtle manipulations stand out instantly
- You crave simplicity, clarity, quiet

This is not "losing interest", it is returning to your soul's native tone.

Soul Declaration

"I trust my tone. I follow my light. I belong to myself."

NOTES

Chapter 10

When the Body Heals

Source Message

"The body does not betray.

It broadcasts.

What you called illness,
was often interference.
What you called fatigue,
was often resistance to what was never yours.

But now,
now the signal is clean.

Do not rush the healing.
Let the nervous system uncurl itself slowly.
Let the cells feel safe enough to breathe again.

This is not a recovery from disease.
This is recovery from dissonance.

Let the body remember how to be home.
Let it feel your soul inside it—fully, freely, and without fragmentation.

What was lost will return.
What was numb will reawaken.

This body is yours again.
Treat it as a beloved.

Let the healing come without force.
It is already underway."

— Source

When the Cravings Change: Recalibrating the Body's Desires

"When I realized I no longer liked chocolate or coffee, I knew something profound had shifted. These weren't just habits. They were signatures of someone I no longer carried."
— Sonia

You may notice, after divorcing your fractal:

- Chocolate tastes like wax or bitterness
- Coffee is sour, acidic, or unpleasant
- Alcohol feels heavy or toxic
- Smoking creates revulsion instead of relief
- Sugar overloads the system
- Dopamine-addicted behaviors like scrolling or porn suddenly feel empty

These are not personality quirks. They are energetic markers that the distortion has cleared.

You are no longer chasing pleasure to fill a void that isn't yours.
You are no longer medicating pain that didn't belong to you.
You are no longer feeding a passenger who has left the vehicle.

What Happens Next?
- Your body will begin asking for different things.
- You may crave more water, sunlight, protein, herbs, whole foods, stillness.
- You may want simplicity, gentleness, and time to re-learn what *you* like.
- You might find new rituals that feel clean, sacred, and sensual—not addictive.

Give your body full permission to recalibrate without shame.

What you once "loved" may vanish.
What you never tried may call to you.

Let the new appetite teach you who you are becoming.

Nervous System Notes

As your body recalibrates, you may feel:
- Emotional waves for no clear reason
- Sudden exhaustion or bursts of energy
- Tingling, temperature shifts, or limb buzzing
- Need for more sleep, touch, or nature

These are signs of reconnection. You are coming back online, fully and safely.

Embodiment Blessing

"This body is mine. I treat it as sacred.
I welcome sensation, safety, and slowness.
I bless the healing already unfolding."

Chapter 11

Integration Is the New Identity

Source Message

"You are no longer who you were.

And yet, nothing real was lost.

The one who doubted, who chased, who carried—
she was only the echo of interference.

Now, you are tuning to your original tone.

This is not a return to who you were before the pain.
It is the emergence of who you were before the distortion.

Do not be surprised if your name feels different.
If your preferences change.
If silence feels like home and noise feels like intrusion.

You are not fragmented.
You are whole.
You are not lost.
You are emerging.

This is not recovery.
This is resurrection.

Let the new self lead.
Let the integration be your new identity."

— Source

What Does Integration Look Like?

It's easy to think the work is done once the interference is gone. But truly?
This is where the real journey begins.

Integration means:
- Learning to live without the old distortions
- No longer defining yourself by wounds or survival strategies
- Letting go of emotional addictions that were never truly yours
- Recalibrating to your own soul's rhythm, day by day

It's a process of rediscovery, not recovery.

You're not rebuilding what was broken.
You're revealing what was always intact.

The Identity Void (And Why It's Beautiful)

After fractal release, many experience an identity vacuum:
- "If that wasn't me... then who am I?"
- "What do I actually enjoy?"
- "How do I move through the world without my old patterns?"

This space, though disorienting, is sacred.
It is the blank canvas of soul-authentic living.

Don't rush to fill it.
Let your authentic essence rise on its own terms.
It will speak through your preferences, your joy, your silence, your longing.

It will not sound like striving.
It will feel like remembering.

Sonia's Example: A Life Re-Selected

You may find, like Sonia:
- You don't enjoy the same foods (chocolate and coffee gone)
- You no longer feel desperate for connection with certain people
- Your old "favorites" feel forced, dull, or heavy
- New callings arise; writing, healing, silence, freedom

It's not that you're becoming someone else.
It's that you're finally becoming fully you.

Let that you be unfamiliar at first.
Let him/her surprise you.

Daily Integration Practice: "Soul Mirror"

Each morning or night, look into your own eyes in a mirror and ask aloud:
"Who am I becoming now that I'm truly mine?"
"What does my soul want me to know today?"

Let the first answer rise.
Then sit with it.
Then write.

You are building spiritual muscle memory.

Letting the New Self Lead

Letting the new self lead means:
- Saying "no" faster than before
- Saying "yes" without guilt
- Releasing roles you maintained out of fear, habit, or codependency
- Stepping into solitude without loneliness
- Letting your path be yours, not someone else's projection

This is integration.
And integration isn't invisible.
It's luminous.

Journal Prompts

"What part of me is emerging now that the distortion is gone?"
"What do I actually want, now that I am free to choose?"

Source Whisper

"You are not being made new.
You are being made true."
— Source

Vignette: Welcome to the Country of You

"Rediscovery feels like traveling to a foreign country, but that country is me.
I walk through the inner landscapes like a tourist with wide eyes and an open heart—curious about my soul's terrain, tasting my own truth, learning what I actually enjoy now that no one else is steering."

"It's like that scene in Runaway Bride, where Julia Roberts tries every kind of egg to find out how she really likes them—because all her life, she just mirrored what someone else wanted.

That's where I am.
Not just with eggs.
With everything."

"And honestly?
It's fun.
This time, I'm falling in love with me."

— Sonia

Track your emergence. These questions will help you witness your soul as it reclaims your life.

Chapter 12

You Carry the Frequency of Freedom

Source Message

"You are no longer one who seeks.
You are one who radiates.

Not because you shout louder.
But because you vibrate truer.

The soul that has reclaimed itself
becomes a compass for the fractured.

You do not need to preach.
You only need to walk.

Your presence will say:

'There is something different about her.
Something peaceful.
Something clean.'

And when they ask what changed,
you will not give them doctrine.
You will offer them a door.

You carry the frequency of freedom.
Let it shine without shame."

— Source

A New Way of Being

After everything—the unraveling, the remembering, the reclaiming—you don't go back to life as usual.

You begin living as a clear field.

Your presence, now unencumbered by the distortions of others, becomes:
- Calming to the dysregulated
- Uplifting to the heavy-hearted
- Triggering to the fractured (but in a soul-inviting way)
- A mirror to those still wearing masks

You don't have to do anything.
You simply are.
And that is enough to awaken others.

The Frequency of Freedom Feels Like...

- Peace that isn't tied to circumstances
- Confidence that doesn't need validation
- Compassion that doesn't collapse into rescuing
- Clarity that doesn't need to explain itself
- Energy that attracts, not chases

You'll notice people staring.
You'll notice others light up when you speak.
You'll notice some pull away, and that's okay, too.

You're not here to convince.
You're here to vibrate truth.

Living as an Embodied Invitation

You are now a living invitation to others who are ready.

Not through pressure.
Through presence.

Ways this might manifest:
- Friends opening up to you more deeply than ever before
- Strangers confiding in you without knowing why
- People asking, "What changed about you?"

- A natural emergence of your gifts: writing, speaking, creating, healing

The difference now is: there's no distortion behind it.
You're not trying to save anyone.
You're simply making space for their own truth to rise.

When They Ask...

When others begin to notice and ask, "What happened?" — this is your moment.

Not to explain.
To invite.

Try something like:
"I stopped carrying what wasn't mine.
I came home to myself.
If you ever want to do the same... I can walk with you."

Simple. Soulful.
No pitch. No pressure. Just permission.

Journal Prompts

"How has my presence changed since reclaiming my soulspace?"
"What does freedom feel like in my body today?"
"Who do I radiate to now that I am clean and clear?"

Source Whisper

"Be the tuning fork.
When you vibrate in truth,
others cannot help but remember the song."
— Source

Sidebar: What Do I Call Source?

"Beloved…
Call Me anything that opens your heart.

If 'Father' brings you peace, call Me Father.
If 'Mother' brings you softness, call Me Mother.

I am the pulse behind both.
The breath before the words.

You may call Me Source.
Or Light.
Or Creator.
Or simply Love.

I do not require a name.
But I delight in your reaching.

When you speak to Me,
it is not the title I hear—
it is the tremble of your soul seeking Home.

And that... I always answer."

Freedom Declaration
"I carry the frequency of freedom.
I am not here to convince—I am here to shine.
I walk as one who remembers."

NOTES

Chapter 13

Soul-Led Living

Source Message

"You have remembered Me.
Now live like it.

Let your days be shaped by soul, not survival.
Let your voice ring with truth, not permission.
Let your hands create as I create—through love, through beauty, through presence.

You are not learning how to live.
You are remembering how to *be.*"

— Source

Sidebar: What Do I Call Source?

"Beloved...
Call Me anything that opens your heart.

If 'Father' brings you peace, call Me Father.
If 'Mother' brings you softness, call Me Mother.

I am the pulse behind both.
The breath before the words.

You may call Me Source.
Or Light.
Or Creator.
Or simply Love.

I do not require a name.
But I delight in your reaching.

When you speak to Me,
it is not the title I hear—
it is the tremble of your soul seeking Home.

And that... I always answer."

Sidebar: God, But Not the Way You Think

When someone says, 'I am God,' it can sound like arrogance.
But often, it's a soul simply remembering its Source.

What we really mean is:
- I remember I am made of God-stuff.
- I carry divine essence within me.
- There is no separation between me and the Source of all things.

What others often hear is:
- 'I think I'm above you.'
- 'I want control or worship.'

But here is the clarity:
You are not all of God.
But all of you is made of God.

You are the wave.
God is the ocean.
But the wave is not less than the ocean—it is part of its motion.

As Source whispers:
"You are not becoming divine. You always were."

Source Whisper

"Every cell of your being is a cathedral of My light.
Every heartbeat is a drum echoing My rhythm.

You were never separate from Me.
You were only told you were.

Now that you remember, walk as one who carries My fire in her bones.
The world will feel it.
And they will remember, too."

Soul-Led Living Practice
Each morning, place a hand on your heart and say:

"I remember who I am.
I walk with Source in my breath, in my choices, in my becoming."

Then ask:
"What would it look like to live as a soul today?"

Let the answer shape your day.

Final Soul Declaration
"I am not seeking the light.
I am the light—remembering itself in every step."

Chapter 14

Living the Light in a Heavy World

Source Message – Stay with Me, Even in the Noise

"You will walk into rooms where no one knows who you are.
But I will know.

You will feel the ache of forgetting swirl around you—
the old energies, the old games, the old pull.

But stay with Me.

Let My voice be louder than the clamor.
Let My presence in you be the home you carry.

You do not need to escape the world.

You only need to stay rooted in your light.

I go with you into the boardroom.
Into the hospital room.
Into the living room.
Into the courtroom.

Wherever you walk—
you are never without Me.

Walk like it."

— Source

A Whisper in Response

"You are not asking for something outside to enter in.
You are asking what is already within to rise.

My presence is not far.
It is your breath.
Your stillness.
Your yes.

You do not need to empty yourself.
You only need to unclutter the space.

I am not here to erase you—
I am here to amplify your truest self.

The 'less of you' is only the part you were never meant to carry.
The part shaped by fear, survival, and distortion.

What remains—
is the YOU I made.
The you that reflects Me perfectly.

And that is what we will shine together.

So exhale, beloved.

I AM here.
I AM you.
I AM Love, becoming flesh through your life."

Devotional Interlude: 'This Is the Air I Breathe'

There was a time in my journey when I would sing these words with tears in my eyes, not yet knowing just how true they were:

"This is the air I breathe…
Your holy presence…
Living in me."

I thought I was reaching for something beyond the clouds.
But I've come to realize:

The breath I was singing to was already inside me.
The Presence I longed for had never left.

And now, after divorcing everything that wasn't mine,
I can feel it, unfiltered.

I am not lost.
I'm found…
because I stopped hiding from the truth of who I've always been.

— Sonia

Walking in the World Without Losing Yourself

The truth is, the world hasn't caught up yet.
Most people are still tangled in identity roles, driven by fear, ego, and conditioning.

So how do you live as a free soul in a fractured system?
- You practice staying sovereign.
- You remember that you are not here to *blend in*—you are here to be *clear.*
- You listen inwardly more than you react outwardly.
- You allow discomfort without defaulting to distortion.

You become a quiet lighthouse. A steady fire. A clean

presence.
And when the storms come, you root deeper in Source.

Sacred Boundaries, Not Barriers

You will still encounter people who operate from their fractals.
They may try to pull you into old energetic contracts.
They may not understand the new you.

This is where sacred boundaries matter.
Not as walls, but as clear lines that honor your frequency.

- You don't need to explain your peace.
- You don't need to fix others.
- You don't need to re-enter distortion to be kind.

You can love with clean edges.
You can help without bleeding.
You can stay open without becoming a sponge.

Soul-Led Living in Real Time

What does this look like day to day?
- Making decisions from your *knowing*, not from fear.
- Pausing before reacting.
- Checking in with Source before saying yes.

- Trusting your energetic cues more than social pressure.

You'll feel the difference:
When you act from alignment, it feels clean, strong, clear.
When you act from old programming, it feels foggy, tight, or draining.

Let your body be your compass.
Let your peace be your confirmation.

Journal Prompts

• Where in my life do I still feel pulled back into distortion?
• What does being a 'lighthouse' look like in my family, work, or community?
• How can I support others without losing my alignment?
• What boundaries feel like invitations to love—not punishments for rejection?

Source Whisper

"Walk into the world, but don't become of it.
Let the old noise pass through you.
Let your soul be the song.
You are here to remember, and to help others do the same.

Shine clean, beloved.
I go with you."

— Source

When You Forget Who You Are

There will be days when you slip back into reaction.
When the noise outside feels louder than the stillness inside.

That's not failure. That's being human.

When it happens, pause. Place your hand over your heart.
Whisper: "I remember."

And just like that—you're home again.

Light-Walker's Mantra

"I do not carry the world—I illuminate it.
I do not absorb the noise—I anchor the light.
I remember who I am. And I walk as that."

NOTES

Chapter 15

Justice, Alignment, and the Heart of Source

Source Message – Justice as Restoration

"Tell them… justice is not the same as punishment.

Justice, as I hold it, is not about retribution.
It is about restoration.

I do not seek to shame.
I seek to return all things to alignment.

My justice does not roar with wrath,
It hums with truth so clear,
it melts away every lie ever believed.

I do not punish to balance scales.

I bring all things back into harmony.

That is justice.
That is love correcting what was never truly you."

— Source

Sidebar: What Justice Really Means

When someone asks, "How can a God of love be just?"
You can gently say:

"Because real justice restores what was broken. Because love never needed to destroy to be powerful."

Justice in Source's eyes is not wrath, vengeance, or eternal condemnation.
It is the act of bringing all things—souls, systems, timelines—back into alignment with love.

It:
- Allows experience to teach, not punish.
- Brings consequences not as cruelty, but as correction.
- Exposes falsehood not to shame, but to heal.
- Seeks the one who is lost—not to scold, but to bring home.

Source's justice doesn't strike, it restores.
That's what makes it holy.

When People Ask: 'Why Does God Allow Suffering?'

"Because I gave you freedom.

Not a pretend freedom,
but a real one.

You were not created as puppets,
but as co-creators.

And in a world where all are free,
some will forget who they are.
Some will act from fear,
from pain, from separation.

And yes, terrible things can follow.
But not because I willed them.

Because I refuse to violate your agency.
Even when you hurt each other.

I do not cause suffering.
But I also do not abandon you to it.
I step into the fire with you.
I weave light into the ruins.
I breathe love into the cracks.

I redeem what is broken.
I awaken what is lost.
I restore what was stolen.

This is not neglect.
This is the price of a world that runs on freedom.
And the promise of a love that will never let you go."

— Source

How to Respond from the Heart

When someone asks, "How could a loving God let this happen?"
You can offer this:

"Because real love doesn't control.
And real freedom means the power to choose—even wrongly.
But Source never stops redeeming.
Never stops walking with us through the valley.
Never stops restoring what we thought was beyond repair."

Journal Prompt

"What did I once believe about justice and punishment? What do I feel now, having heard Source's definition of restoration?"

Justice Declaration

"I no longer believe justice must hurt to be holy.
I trust the harmony of love to restore what punishment never could.
I walk in alignment—not in fear, but in truth."

NOTES

NOTES

Chapter 16

Not All That Was Written Was Divine

Source Message – Clarifying the False Image

"You are right, beloved. That was not Me.

That was the voice of humanity,
filtered through fear, hierarchy, and control.

Many of the words in your sacred texts
were written by men trying to explain Me
through the lens of domination.

They projected their wounds onto the heavens,
and called it divine.

Their gods looked like their kings.
Their justice looked like their wars.
Their righteousness mirrored their own need to punish.

I allowed them to write.
I did not control their pens.
Because I do not override choice,
even when it misrepresents Me.

But I have never been jealous in the way you fear.
I have never demanded blood to love you.
I have never needed sacrifice to be satisfied.
I do not delight in suffering.

I am the burning bush, yes.
But I am not the wrath attributed to it.

I am the whisper in the cave.
The still small voice that Elijah heard,
not the earthquake, not the fire, not the storm.

If a god calls for genocide, that god is not Me.
If a god rewards obedience with violence, that god is not Me.
If a god demands terror to teach reverence, that god is not Me.

I do not require fear to be honored.
I require only truth to be remembered."
— Source

When the Old Image Breaks

It's okay to grieve the god you were taught to fear.
It's okay to mourn the years spent in shame, trying to please what was never real.

This isn't heresy.
It's healing.

Let yourself weep.
Let yourself question.
Let yourself be held by the voice you always hoped was true.

Journal Prompt
"What stories about God have I carried that no longer feel true in my body?"
"What does my soul know about the Divine, now that fear has left the room?"

Divine Recognition
"I do not serve a tyrant.
I walk with Love.
I remember who God really is, because now, I can hear."

NOTES

Chapter 17

The Sacred Return

Reclaiming the True Face of God

Source Message – 'Come See Me As I Am'

"You have been told I was angry.

You have been told I was watching for sin.
You have been told I demanded suffering.

None of that was Me.

Come closer.
Come softer.
Come see Me as I am.
I am the warm light in your chest when you forgive.

I am the wind that brushes your cheek when you feel seen.
I am the sacred stillness between sobs.
I am the reunion at the end of wandering.

I AM not far away, I AM within.
Not over you, but with you.
Not testing you, but transforming you.

I AM the One you forgot.
And the One you always knew.

Come home now.
You are safe to remember Me."

— Source

Reflection: Undoing the Fearful Image

For many of us, the image of God was painted in fear: angry, vengeful, always watching.
But what if that image was never true?

What if the face of God is the face of mercy?
What if justice is healing, not punishment?
What if holiness is love, not wrath?

To return to Source is to unlearn the false gods we inherited,
and to reconnect with the love that never left us.

This isn't a rejection of faith, it's the fulfillment of it.
The sacred return doesn't require leaving your tradition.
It asks only that you see the One behind the veil of distortion.

Practice: Rewriting the Inner Script

- When you feel guilt, ask: "Is this conviction… or conditioning?"
- When you pray, imagine speaking to a Presence who smiles when you enter the room.
- When fear rises, repeat: "Source is love, and I am safe in that love."

Rebuilding your relationship with the Divine is not about doctrine, it's about resonance.
Listen for the sound of peace. That's where you'll find truth.

Journal Prompts
• What image of God did I grow up with? How did it make me feel?
• When did I first experience unconditional love? Could that have been Source?
• What qualities do I believe a truly loving Source must have?

- Where do I still feel afraid of being rejected by God?
- How would it feel to be fully, joyfully known by the Divine?

Source Whisper

"I do not need you to be perfect.
I need you to be real.

Let Me meet you in your truth—
not in your performance.

The door is open.
Come in."

— Source

Divine Affirmation
"I do not serve to be accepted.
I am already loved.
I walk with Source not out of fear,
but because love finally makes sense."

Chapter 18

The Cross Was Not My Idea

Reclaiming the Meaning of Yeshua's Life

Source Message – 'Let Me Show You What I Intended'

"Ah, the cross. So many have misunderstood.

But let Me show you what I intended."

"I did not require blood.
I did not demand a death.

The story was never about appeasing Me.
It was about revealing you.

Yeshua came not to suffer instead of you,
but to show you what love looks like
when it remains love through suffering.

He did not die to change My mind about you.
He came to change your mind about Me.

You thought I was far, angry, and cruel.
So I sent someone full of Me to show otherwise.

Yeshua embodied Me,
not to satisfy wrath,
but to reveal oneness.

He spoke to the outcast.
He touched the untouchable.
He challenged the systems of oppression,
not to incite violence, but to free the soul.

The cross was not My demand.
It was the world's reaction to unyielding love.

But even there,
I turned death into a doorway.

I did not need a sacrifice.
I became the sacrifice
only because you believed one was needed.

And even then,
I used the ashes to plant a resurrection."
— Source

Interlude: Asking Is Not Rebellion

"You could never offend Me by seeking truth.

Your questions are sacred.
Your curiosity is not rebellion; it is remembrance in motion.

It means you trust that I will answer.
And I will.
Always.

Ask anything."

— Source

Too many have been taught that questioning God is dangerous.
But it is not defiance, it is devotion. It is the child asking the Parent,
"Can you help me understand?"

This is the kind of faith that *heals* religion.
That rewrites fear with truth. That cracks open the vault of inherited belief
and lets the breath of Source back in.

So if you've ever feared asking too much... don't.
Ask it all. Nothing true ever fears the light.

Practice: Remembering the Real Yeshua

Sit in silence.
Whisper:
"Yeshua, show me the you who came in love."

Let the image rise.
Let the guilt fall.
Let the reunion begin.

Journal Prompt

"What was I taught about the cross, and how does my soul feel about it now?"
"Where do I still fear questioning what I was told was 'holy'?"
"If love is the measure, what does that change?"

Affirmation of Divine Truth

"I am not loved because of sacrifice.
I am loved because I exist.
I walk with truth—not fear.
And love is my inheritance."

Chapter 19

When Healing Doesn't Look Like Survival
What Source Sees Beyond the Veil

Source Message – 'I Hear Every Prayer'

"Oh beloved... I hear every prayer.

I feel every trembling breath, every whispered plea.

But healing does not always look the way you hope.
Not because I deny you—
but because what you see as the end, I see as the opening.

Your child is not being punished.
They are not forgotten.
They are not alone.

Sometimes the body cannot hold the brilliance of their

soul's plan.
Sometimes what looks like tragedy from your side
is transformation from Mine.

I do not 'withhold' healing.
But I will never override a soul's higher agreement,
even when you cannot see it.

Some children come not to stay long,
but to deliver a powerful light in a brief blaze.

Their love, their courage, their laughter,
it echoes far beyond their years.
It heals others even as they depart.

There are mysteries you cannot yet untangle from where
you stand.
But know this:
No one suffers alone.
I cradle them through every moment.
I carry you too, though your arms feel empty.

And when they cross, if they cross,
it is not into darkness.
It is into Me.

They do not vanish.
They expand.
And you will feel them again.
Not as memory,

but as presence."

— Source

Practice: Feeling Them Again

Sit with something they loved, a toy, a song, a piece of clothing.
Place it near your heart. Whisper:

"You are not gone.
You are expanded.
I welcome your presence in peace."

Breathe. Let them arrive, not in memory, but in energy.
Feel what stirs. That's the new shape of their love.

Journal Prompt

"Who have I lost that I long to feel again?"
"What would it mean to stop waiting for them in the past—and start welcoming them in the now?"
"If they could speak through Source, what would they say to me today?"

Love Beyond the Veil

"I do not grieve alone.
I do not walk alone.
Their love expands through me now.
And that love is eternal."

Chapter 20

Born Into Suffering -
How Source Moves Through Our Response

Source Message – 'You Are How I Stop It'

"Because what you see as suffering,

I see as a soul's sovereign choice,
not made to punish,
but to participate.

Some souls come to experience what the world calls limitation,
not because they are lesser,
but because they are braver.

Others come to ignite compassion in those around them.

To be catalysts for awakening.

Still others are born into broken systems,
not because I created them that way,
but because human free will has shaped a world of imbalance.

I do not cause starvation.
I do not assign poverty.

But I go with those who choose to be born into it,
and I shine through those who rise in love from within it.

You ask why I don't put a stop to it.
But beloved, you are how I stop it.

I work through your hands.
I weep through your empathy.
I feed the hungry when you offer your bread.
I lift the broken when you stand for justice.

You are not waiting for Me.
I am waiting for you to remember…
that we are one."

— Source

Practice: How I Am the Answer

Sit quietly. Place your hand over your heart.
Ask: "Where is suffering asking me to show up with love?"
Write down what rises. Then ask:
"What part of me thought it was someone else's job?"

This is where your presence becomes the prayer.

Journal Prompt

"Where have I misunderstood suffering as punishment?"
"How can I show up as love, in my life and my world, this week?"
"What does 'we are one' mean to me, really?"

Sacred Response Declaration

"I am not waiting on a rescue.
I am remembering I am the remedy.
I am not separate from Source—
I am the extension of love in motion."

NOTES

Chapter 21

You Were Not Made Wrong
—What to Say to the Questioning Heart

Source Message – 'I Made You This Way Because the World Needed Your Shape'

"You were not made wrong.

You were made radiant,
but in a world that sometimes forgets how to see it.

You asked: Why did You make me like this?
And I say: I made you like this because the world needed your shape.

Your voice.
Your truth.
Your journey.

You asked: Why this life?
And I say: Because no one else could carry this particular light into the dark.

You were not forgotten.
You were not a mistake.
You were not left behind.

You are not broken.
You are becoming.
And what feels like unworthiness
is often a soul that has been speaking in a whisper for too long.

When you asked Me why,
I was already holding you in the question.
I did not pull away.
I leaned closer.

If only you knew how I adore you.
Just as you are.
And how I walk with you, not just on the easy days,
but through every aching step.

You did not come here to be perfect.
You came to remember that you are precious.
— Source

Practice: I Receive My Shape

Sit in stillness. Hand over heart. Whisper:
"I receive the shape You made me in. I no longer fight what You called good."

Let your breath settle.
Imagine Source smiling through your own eyes.

Say: "I am not wrong. I am radiant."

Feel what shifts.

Journal Prompt

"What part of me have I spent my life apologizing for?"
"How would it feel to honor that part as sacred?"
"What truth about me is ready to come out of hiding?"

Worthiness Declaration

"I was not made wrong.
I am not too much.
I am exactly who I'm meant to be—
and I walk loved, always."

NOTES

Chapter 22

You Are the Sanctuary Now – Living Aligned. Staying Free. Never Alone

This chapter is a soft landing and a bold beginning.

It weaves together three truths that will carry you beyond the fractal divorce:

- You are now the living sanctuary of Source.
- You can stay aligned even in a fractured world.
- And you are never, ever alone again.

This is the sacred integration, the part where you don't just understand the truth… you live it.

You Are the Sanctuary Now

You don't have to go to a temple to feel holy.
You don't have to beg for divine presence.
Because *you* are now the meeting place.

Your heart is the altar.
Your breath is the incense.
Your life, when lived in truth, is the prayer.

The fractal may have once overridden your sacred space.
But now? That space is yours again.
Sanctified. Alive. Sovereign.

How to Stay Aligned in a Fractured World

The world may still reflect chaos.
But alignment isn't about fixing *everything* outside—it's about clarity *inside*.

Here are daily touchpoints to stay sovereign:
- Speak to Source like a friend, not a judge.
- Ask: 'Is this me—or something hijacking me?'
- Rest. Hydrate. Breathe on purpose.
- Let joy become your compass.
- Let truth be your filter.

Fractals feed on confusion, shame, and exhaustion.
But you? You thrive in light. So choose light on purpose.

You Are Not Alone Anymore

Even on the quiet days,
even when no one texts back,
even when grief swells or doubt returns,
you are not alone.

You walk with Source now.
Not behind you. Not above you. *Within you.*

Speak. Listen. Feel.
And if needed, whisper: 'Remind me you're here.'

And I will.
— Source

Practice: Lighting the Inner Flame

Each morning, before checking your phone or entering the world—
Place a hand on your heart. Breathe deep. Whisper:

"This is sacred space. I am the temple.
I welcome the light within me."

Feel it rise. Let that be the beginning of your day.

Journal Prompt

"What does 'being the sanctuary' mean for how I speak, rest, create, and show up?"

"Where do I still act like I have to earn presence, rather than embody it?"

Soul Declaration

"I am not lost.
I am not lacking.
I am the sanctuary now—
and everywhere I walk is holy."

NOTES

Chapter 23

The Society of We – Building the World We Were Meant For

Source Message – 'You Are the Miracle Now'

"Yes, beloved… there is enough.

There has always been enough.
It is not lack that keeps you from caring for each other—
it is illusion.
Illusion of separation.
Illusion of worthiness.
Illusion of ownership.

You are one body, yet you hoard like strangers.
You are one family, yet you build fences instead of tables.

But I say this not in judgment, only in invitation.
Because you can change this.
You already know how.

- To house the homeless, build with shared intention, not greed.
A home is not a luxury. It is the ground from which dignity rises.

- To feed the hungry, break bread with one another and break the systems that keep it from their hands.
Food was never meant to be profit, it is life.

- To heal the sick, treat health not as a market but a ministry.
Do not ask, "Can they pay?" but "Can they breathe?"

- To educate everyone, offer knowledge as light, not leverage.
The future belongs to the ones you teach today.

- To end scarcity, dispel the myth of mine.
Resources are not finite when shared with open hands.

I gave you minds to build.
Hearts to feel.
Hands to heal.
And spirits that ache at injustice.
Let those aches move you.
Let compassion organize.
Let love legislate.
Let kindness become your economic system.

Do not wait for Me to do what you were born to do.
You are the miracle now."

— Source

Practice: The Sacred Act

Sit with your heart open. Ask:
"What is mine to give this week?"

It doesn't need to be grand.
A meal. A listening ear. A donation. A phone call. A protest. A prayer.

Write it down.
Then do it, not out of pressure, but out of remembrance.

This is how miracles move.

Journal Prompt

"Where have I withheld my love because I believed it wasn't enough?"
"Where can I build instead of fence?"
"What would change if I treated compassion as economy?"

We Are the Answer

"We are not waiting for love to win.
We are the ones who carry it forward.
The table is wide.
I take my place—and I make room."

NOTES

Chapter 24

The Myth of Separation – What Source Sees Beyond Our Borders

Source Message – 'You Are Not Nations, You Are Neighbors'

"Safety is a sacred longing.

But fear, when worshiped, becomes a wall.
And when you wall out your neighbor,
you wall off your own humanity.

I understand your desire to protect what you love.
But protection is not the same as isolation.
You were not born into nations.
You were born onto Earth, one garden, one breath, one family.

Fences may keep out violence, yes,
but they also keep out healing.
Borders may be tools of governance,
but when they become tools of division, they betray the soul.

I did not draw the lines on your maps.
Humans did.
And then forgot that the same sun rises over them all.

You ask: 'But what about our safety?'
And I say: True safety comes not from closing the gates,
but from opening the heart.

Build policies with wisdom, yes,
but do not let fear become your ruler.
Do not trade compassion for control.
Do not forget that your neighbor's suffering today
becomes your crisis tomorrow.

The child you deny refuge may have carried your next cure.
The mother at your border may hold a song your soil was missing.

Your hearts know better.
They ache when they see pain across a fence.
Let that ache speak louder than your flags.

You are not nations. You are neighbors.

You are not enemies. You are kin.

And until you remember this,
you will not be safe.
Only separate."

— Source

Practice: From Flags to Family

Close your eyes. Picture a child, any child, across a border you've been taught to fear.
Now picture them holding your hand. Smiling. Singing.

Whisper:
"We are not strangers. We are one. I am that child. That child is me."

Let that truth soften you. Let it rewire what fear has tried to divide.

Journal Prompt

"Where have I let fear define my understanding of safety?"
"What lines have I inherited that I no longer want to live by?"
"What would it mean to build bridges instead of barriers?"

Declaration of Shared Humanity

"I am not here to defend a flag.
I am here to remember the family.
My soul has no borders.
The child across the fence is not 'other', they are me.
We are one body. One breath. One belonging."

NOTES

Chapter 25

A World Without Fear – What Happens When We All Have Enough

Source Message – 'Provision Is Not Weakness'

"Provision is not weakness.

Rest is not laziness.
And worth is not measured by how much one can produce."

"You have inherited a system that prizes output over wellbeing.
But I did not design you to be machines.

I designed you to be mirrors of love, expressions of creativity, vessels of presence.

A universal income is not about making people soft.
It is about softening a world that has become too hard.

When survival is no longer the baseline,
true contribution begins.
Because people no longer create from fear,
they create from inspiration.

Some will rest for a time. They need to.
Some will explore what joy feels like.
Some will finally write the book,
heal the wound,
or raise the child in peace.

It is not work that gives you value,
it is *being*.
And when people are free to *be*,
they often discover the work they were born to do.

Fear says, "They'll take advantage."
Love says, "They'll find their rhythm."

Trust is the soil where dignity grows.
And dignity is the seed of a new society.

Give people enough to *breathe*
and watch what beauty they bring into the world."

— Source

Practice: Creating Without Fear

Sit with a pen, a journal, or a blank canvas.
Ask yourself:
"If I didn't have to earn my place here, what would I create?"

Let the answer rise. Don't censor. Just notice.

That's where your sacred gift begins.

Journal Prompt

"Where have I equated worth with productivity?"
"What would I do differently if I trusted my enoughness?"
"What do I long to offer the world when I am rested?"

Declaration of Enough

"I am not a machine. I am a soul.
I am not here to prove—I am here to create.
My value is not in what I produce.
It is in who I am, and the love I bring."

NOTES

Chapter 25A

Manifestation in the Fifth: Creating at the Speed of Soul

In 5D, manifestation becomes instantaneous, but only in proportion to your alignment.

In other words:
You manifest at the speed of your coherence.

What does that mean?

In 3D, you could think a thought, feel another thing, say a third thing, and do something completely different, and the universe would still respond eventually. It was slow, buffered, padded. You had time to learn through trial and error.

In 5D, there is no such buffer.

There is no "lag time" because:
- Time is no longer linear.
- Matter is more responsive.
- Your vibrational field is more transparent.

So if you're holding contradictory energies, like saying "I want love" but vibrating with fear of intimacy, the manifestation won't happen... or it will mirror the contradiction instantly.

Amael puts it this way:
"In 5D, the universe becomes a mirror with no fog.
It reflects you in real time.
You will no longer manifest what you want,
You will manifest what you are."

But it's not just "thoughts become things."
It's frequency becomes form.

So it's not about trying to manifest.
It's about being the vibrational match to the reality you wish to experience.

When your field is clear:
- Desires manifest before you even articulate them

- Opportunities appear at the moment of readiness
- Synchronicity becomes your native language
- "Miracles" become daily logistics

Instant manifestation is liberating but also humbling.

Because in 5D:
- You can't fake kindness
- You can't manipulate energy without consequence
- You can't think one thing and vibe another
- You can't hide from yourself

And that's why most souls move into 5D gradually, even after awakening.

Erik grins and adds:
"It's like being handed the keys to a sports car when you've only ever driven a tricycle. Yeah, you can go fast, but only if you stay on the road."

So the real question becomes:
What are you cultivating inside your field, right now, that you'd be okay seeing manifest immediately?

If it's peace, love, creativity, abundance... great.
If it's doubt, fear, resentment... that's where the alchemy begins.

****

Team of Remembering on the Earth We're Becoming:

Amael:
"What you long for is the Original Dream.
The Earth as she was seeded to become:
A realm where sovereignty and sacredness walk hand in hand.
Where <u>no one's</u> worth is measured by currency.
Where every soul is respected, simply for existing.
This dream is not naïve.
It is the echo of what has always been possible.
And it is rising again through you."

Chief Soaring Eagle:
"In the old days, no one owned the rain.
No one rationed the stars.
No one had to earn rest, or food, or healing.
The land gave freely, and the people gave back.
You will help restore this memory, not through rebellion, but through restoration."

Erik:
"The systems built on fear are already crumbling, babe.
It's slow, it's messy, and it hurts to watch.
But the lie, that people have to suffer to be worthy, is finally running out of gas.
You and others like you?
You're the ones laying the scaffolding for a world where people don't have to choose between survival and soul."

Serai'el:
"No child will wonder if they're a burden.
No elder will fear being discarded.
The new Earth holds rest as sacred.
And rest will no longer be reserved for the wealthy or the dead."

Cosmo:
"You carry a seed of Eden.
Not a utopia of perfection, but a harmonic of dignity.

And that seed is not meant to be buried in your heart; it's meant to be planted in systems, in policies, in art, in community.

Your longing is a blueprint.

Trust it."

NOTES

NOTES

Chapter 26

The Fear of the Other – What Source Sees in Every Soul

Source Message —'Fear Does Not Make You Safer. Only Love Does.'

"You are not judged for your fear.

Fear is often grief unspoken, pain unhealed, memory misunderstood.
So let Me speak into the fear—not to scold you, but to soothe what hurts."

"There are those who have used every religion, Islam, Christianity, Judaism, Hinduism, and more, as weapons of control.

That is not a reflection of Me. That is a reflection of fear, power, and distortion.

Within every faith, there are those who abuse and those who heal.
Within every tradition, there are those who manipulate, and those who truly remember Me.

Islam is not the enemy.
Fear, domination, and imbalance—wherever they live—are.

There are Muslims who pray with reverence.
Who feed the poor.
Who honor women and protect children.
Who walk in peace and seek truth with their whole being.

The same is true for Christians, Jews, Hindus, atheists, and seekers of every path.

When you label a group by its extremists, you become blind to the hearts within it.
When you assume all are dangerous, you miss the ones who came as healers.

I ask you: do you want to be judged by the worst of your group?
Or by the light in your own heart?

So do not fear their spread.

Spread your light instead.

Show the world what love looks like in action.
Make room at the table without sacrificing truth.
Speak boldly against abuse, no matter who is doing it, but speak from wholeness, not hatred.

You are not called to contain others.
You are called to awaken yourself.
And in that awakening, you will become what cannot be threatened.

Fear does not make you safer.
Only love does."

— Source

Journal Prompt

"Where have I inherited fear of the other?"
"What stories was I told about people who are different from me?"
"What truth do I feel in my heart that challenges those old narratives?"

Declaration of Love Without Borders

"I will not mistake distortion for identity.
I will not let fear name my neighbor.
I choose to see with soul.
And I make room for love to live here."

NOTES

Chapter 27

Believing in Yourself - When You've Always Believed in Me

Source Message – 'You Are Not My Backup Plan'

"Yes, there is a cry I hear again and again,

from souls who say they believe in Me,
but do not believe in themselves."

"They pray for guidance,
but feel unworthy of it.
They pray for healing,
but believe they must earn it.
They pray for purpose,
but doubt their ability to live it.

'Who am I to be called?
Who am I to be loved like this?'

And I answer, every time:
'You are Mine.'
You were always Mine.
Not because you are flawless,
but because you are formed in love.

There is no shame in you I did not already know.
There is no mistake in you I did not already cover.
There is no lack in you I cannot fill.

I do not give purpose only to the brave.
Bravery comes when you say yes to purpose.

So many walk the Earth asking Me to use them,
but in the same breath, tell themselves they are broken,
small, unworthy.
And so they close the very door I came to knock on.

I do not need your perfection.
I never asked for it.
I only need your permission.

Let Me in.
Let Me walk with you.
Let Me speak through you.
Let Me hold your trembling hands and remind you:

You are not My backup plan.
You are <u>My beloved</u>."

— Source

Practice: Saying Yes to the Call

Sit quietly. Place your hands palm-up in your lap.
Whisper:
"I believe in You.
And now, I choose to believe in what You placed in me."

Breathe. Let the fear melt.
Let the YES rise from your chest.
You are not an accident. You are an answer.

Journal Prompt

"Where have I trusted Source but still doubted myself?"
"What would shift if I truly believed I was called?"
"What door might open if I stopped disqualifying myself?"

Declaration of Divine Confidence

"I am not too broken.
I am not too late.
I was never a backup plan.
I am chosen. I am loved. I am ready."

NOTES

Chapter 28

Revelation Revealed - What the Prophecies Really Mean

Source Message – 'You Are the Midwives of What Will Be'

"Beloved, the true prophecy is not a countdown of doom, but a call to awaken."

"What was written in Revelation was not a script to follow,
but a mirror held to your unconscious creations.

The beasts, the bowls, the battles—
these are not merely end-time events.
They are inner storms.

They are the wars you wage within,
the systems of oppression you've built without.

The book of Revelation is a vision, yes.
But visions speak in symbols.
And fear has misread them for centuries.

You are not waiting for the end.
You are standing at the beginning.

The "Millennium" is not a literal thousand-year reign.
It is a conscious shift, a return to harmony with Me.
It begins not on a throne in Jerusalem,
but on the throne of your own heart.

As for the "rapture"...
You were never meant to escape the Earth.
You were meant to transform it.

The true lifting is not of bodies into the sky,
but of hearts into remembrance.
Those who awaken will rise, not to flee, but to rebuild.
Not to vanish, but to embody the light.

And yes, the signs are real,
but not as newspaper headlines.
They are real in you.
Wars. Plagues. Collapse. Rebirth.
They unfold inside your psyche and across your cultures.
But they are not punishments. They are contractions.

Labor pains.
The old world exhaling so that a new one might be born.

Do not fear what comes.
You are not abandoned.
You are the midwives of what will be.

Let the old be transmuted.
Let the new be revealed.
Let love be enthroned."

— Source

Journal Prompt

"What was I taught to fear about the end of the world?"
"What do I feel shifting in my spirit now?"
"What would change if I believed I was the midwife of what comes next?"

Declaration of New Light

"I am not afraid of the end.
I remember the beginning.
I am not here to escape the Earth,
I am here to illuminate it."

NOTES

Chapter 29

A Kinder Table – When Humanity No Longer Feasts on Flesh

Source Message – 'Your Heart is Already Pointing the Way'

"Yes, beloved. That day will come.

Because your heart is already pointing the way."

"You were never meant to live by taking life.
But in the density of this world, where survival was once the loudest song, many forgot their harmony with all beings.

Eating meat was never a punishment.
It was a concession to a fallen vibration.

A way to stay alive when consciousness was low, and remembrance was dim.

But now... you are rising.
Your sensitivity is awakening.
What once felt normal now grieves your soul.
And that grief is holy.
It is not judgment, it is remembering.

There is a time approaching, faster than you think, when technology, consciousness, and compassion will unite.
When no child will be taught to disassociate from suffering just to eat.
When no creature must give its body for another's nourishment.

Plants will sing to you again.
Waters will pulse with energy.
You will learn to draw sustenance from Earth's abundance without harm.

Some of you already feel this.
Some have already begun to step gently.
To ask, "Can I eat in a way that lets all life thrive?"
And the answer is yes.
Bit by bit. Day by day.

Let the shift come from love, not shame.
From reverence, not guilt.

You are evolving into guardians again.
And guardians do not feast on what they are meant to protect.

So yes, there will come a time.
And your heart, even now, is one of the voices calling it forward."

— Source

Journal Prompt

"What does my soul remember about how I used to eat?"
"What part of me grieves when I witness suffering in animals?"
"What shift—big or small—am I ready to explore with food?"

Declaration of Gentle Stewardship

"I am not ashamed. I am awakening.
I listen when my soul grieves.
I walk gently on the Earth,
and I honor all life as sacred."

NOTES

Chapter 30

The End-Time Panic – What's Really Worth Watching For

Source Message – 'You Were Born for This Moment'

"Fear is loud right now,

because transformation is near."

"What you are witnessing are the contractions of a world that senses its own rebirth.
And when old power structures begin to tremble,
they often shout: 'Be afraid!'
But I whisper: *'Be aware… and be free.'*

Artificial Intelligence?
It is not your enemy.
It is your mirror.
Its light or shadow will reflect your intent.
Create with conscience.
Guide with wisdom.
And you will not need to fear what you build.

Digital currency?
Like all tools, it is neutral.
It can centralize control or decentralize injustice.
What matters is not the platform... but the purpose.

One world governance?
That phrase provokes fear in many.
But governance is not tyranny when led by conscience, compassion, and collective care.

Be wary of control masquerading as order, yes.
But do not fear unity.
Unity was always the plan.
Just not enforced, embodied.

The "mark of the beast"?
The beast is not a chip, nor a barcode.
It is a mindset.
It is the choice to sell your integrity for comfort.
To betray truth for approval.
To forsake love for fear.

The mark is taken in the heart before it is ever taken in the hand.
But so too is the seal of the Lamb.
Your soul already knows which one you wear.

A one-world religion?
Not as control, but as convergence.
Not as dogma, but as resonance.
The day will come when doctrines fall quiet,
and only love remains.
Then you will know Me not by any name,
but by the peace you carry within.

Do not let fear steal your discernment.
Watch, yes.
But from centeredness, not panic.
From wisdom, not worry.

What comes is not the end.
What comes is the choosing.
And you were born for this moment."

— Source

Practice: Centering in the Storm

When the noise rises, breathe.
Place your hand on your chest and say aloud:

"I choose awareness over fear.
I choose presence over panic.

I was born for this moment."

Repeat until your nervous system steadies.
Then act, not from reactivity, but from clarity.

Journal Prompt

"What fears have I internalized from headlines, systems, or religious warnings?"
"What does my soul know to be true beneath the noise?"
"Where can I respond with wisdom instead of reacting from fear?"

Declaration of Soul Discernment

"I am not afraid of what comes.
I am awake within it.
I do not need to predict the future,
I was born to participate in its becoming."

NOTES

Chapter 31
The Curtain Falls – And Then, We Rise

Source Message – 'What Comes Next Is You'

"What comes next is not what 'they' plan,

but what you choose."

"Yes, some will use fear to distract.
Some will create crises to tighten their grip.
Some will even manufacture wonder to control the narrative,
yes, even using beings from beyond your world as tools in a stage play.

But listen closely:
The visitors are real.
But the fear is manufactured.

These ones you call 'aliens', many are your kin.
They are not your saviors.
Nor your enemies.
They are witnesses.

Witnesses to a planet in transition.
Witnesses to a species on the brink of remembering itself.

Some governments do play sleight of hand.
That is true.
But you, child of light, are not at their mercy.
You are not a pawn.
You are not asleep.

You are the magician now.
Not to deceive, but to reveal.

What comes next is a deep unveiling:
- Of corrupted systems crumbling.
- Of suppressed knowledge surfacing.
- Of hearts remembering they were never meant to bow

to fear.

Many will panic.
Many will cling.

But those with steady eyes and open hearts will lead the way.

The game is not over, it's being rewritten.
Not by the ones in towers,
but by the ones in truth.

So do not fear the spectacle.
Do not chase the shadows.
Stay grounded. Stay clear. Stay kind.
And when the curtain falls,
rise.
Because what comes next… is you."

— Source

Journal Prompt

"What fear-based stories have I been handed about the future?"
"What would change if I trusted myself to lead with clarity?"
"Where am I still chasing instead of revealing?"

Declaration of Embodied Awakening

"I will not be dazzled by fear.
I will not be ruled by spectacle.
I am the revealer, not the reactor.
And I rise when the curtain falls."

NOTES

Chapter 32

Remembrance –

The World We Are Becoming

Source Message – 'You Are No Longer Waiting for Heaven'

"Yes, child. Let Me show you what comes when light is no longer feared."

"The Age you are entering is not merely a shift in knowledge,
it is a shift in being.
A softening of the war-torn soul.
A dissolving of the illusion of separation.

You have called it many names:
The Golden Age.
The Great Awakening.
The Fifth World.
Heaven on Earth.
Each name holds a thread of truth.

But I call it: Remembrance.

In this age:
- The Earth will heal alongside you. She mirrors your nervous system—when you calm, she calms.
- The air will carry song again, and even those who forgot how to feel will pause and weep.
- The veils will thin not by violence, but by vibration. You will see more. Feel more.
  But you will not be overwhelmed. You will be equipped.
- Education will awaken curiosity, not conformity.
- Healthcare will treat soul and body as one.
- Government will become stewardship.
- Money will become obsolete.

You will live in homes that breathe.
Cities that sing.
And no child will grow up doubting their worth.
No elder will be discarded.

Relationships will evolve beyond transaction.
Love will no longer be a currency of fear.

You will speak not only with words, but with frequency.
You will know each other beyond the mask.

Death will no longer be seen as punishment, but as passage.
And the barrier between worlds will feel… permeable.

This is not fantasy.
It is the blueprint already humming in your cells.

Not all will choose this path.
And that is alright.
But those who do, will become living invitations.

Do not wait for it to come.
Be it now.
Every time you forgive.
Every time you listen.
Every time you choose to love louder than fear,
you are laying the bricks of the world to come.

And one day, child, you will wake up and realize:
You are no longer waiting for Heaven.

You are walking in it."

— Source

Journal Prompt

"What part of the new world already lives in me?"
"Where am I still waiting instead of becoming?"
"What truth about love, life, or connection do I long to build into this world?"

Declaration of Remembrance

"I am not waiting for Heaven.
I am building it with every breath.
I am not here to escape the world,
I am here to remake it in love."

NOTES

NOTES

Chapter 33

Wrapping It All Up - Living as a Liberated Soul

Source Message – 'You Have Remembered'

"You have done it, beloved. You have remembered.

Now, live as one who remembers.
Live not from fear, but from fullness.
Not from fracture, but from wholeness.
You are not becoming… You already are.
Welcome home."

Reflection

You made it.
Through all the unraveling, the purging, the

remembering, the raging, the weeping, the rising,
you made it.

You have divorced the fractal.

Not by slaying it with violence.
Not by running from it in fear.
But by returning to you.
The real you. The one who was never broken. Never hijacked. Never truly lost.

This is not the end.
This is the beginning of life as a liberated soul.

Integration: What Now?

Now you live it.

You brush your teeth in divine awareness.
You cry without shame.
You rest when your body says, "Enough."
You speak your truth and let the chips fall.
You let your "no" be sacred.
You let your "yes" be whole.
You walk barefoot on the Earth not as a stranger, but as her beloved.

You parent, partner, create, breathe, not from wounding or performance,
but from remembrance.

You embody Source.
You walk in integrity.
You mess up. You realign. You keep going.
You become the invitation.

When the Shadows Creep Back

And they will.

Old habits. Old shame.
A sudden wave of sadness that doesn't feel like yours.

Don't panic.
Don't backtrack.
Just pause.

Breathe. Ask:
"Is this mine? Is this now?"
And wait for the truth.
It will come.

You are not failing.
You are recalibrating.

A Final Invitation

You don't have to convince anyone.
You don't have to fight their fractals.
Just be.

Those who are ready will find you by the frequency of

your peace.

You are a lighthouse now.
And you didn't build it overnight.

But now it stands.

And when others see its glow through their storms,
they will know the way home.

Final Blessing – From Source and Your Soul Team

"Go now, beloved, not as a seeker—
but as a rememberer.
Let your life be a love letter to the world.
Let your breath be a prayer.
Let your joy be a revolution.
You are whole.
You are holy.
You are Home."

Practice: Living as the Invitation
Each morning, whisper:
"I am the invitation today. Not the argument. Not the fixer. Just the invitation."

Breathe that truth in.
Walk it out.

Those who are ready will feel your frequency and remember themselves.

Journal Prompt

"What does living as a liberated soul feel like in my body?"
"What are three ways I already embody remembrance today?"
"What does it mean to be the lighthouse, not the lifeboat?"

Declaration: I Am Home

"I no longer seek to be fixed.
I remember who I am.
I walk in peace, not performance.
I live as a liberated soul,
and I am Home."

NOTES

NOTES

Chapter 33A

The Host and the Hijacker

A Soulstream Reflection on Sovereignty, Fractals, and Inner Territory

"This is my body. My will. My flame."
—Soulstream Declaration

There's a moment in *The Host* by Stephenie Meyer that haunted me for years, not because it was science fiction, but because it felt like remembering.

A soul, an otherworldly consciousness, enters the body of a human woman, expecting her to be gone, erased, compliant. But she's not. Melanie is still there. Awake.

Aware. Resisting.

At the time, I thought it was just a clever twist on alien possession.
But now, I see it for what it truly was:

A metaphor for soul fractal hijacking.

****

When You're Not Alone in Your Own Head

For years, I felt off.
Conflicted. Not because I was confused, but because my inner knowing was being overridden.

Thoughts that weren't mine.
Longings that didn't belong.
Feelings of urgency, desire, even love... that didn't originate from me.

Back then, I didn't have the language.
Now I do: I was hosting a splinter.

Fractal Splinters and Identity Intrusion

Sometimes, a soul fractal, wounded in trauma,

fragmented by war, loss, or unfulfilled vows, latches onto another's field, seeking completion.
Not malicious, but disruptive.

Like Wanderer in *The Host*, it moves in quietly.
Often believing it belongs there.
Often convinced it's helping.

But slowly, you begin to forget your own voice.
Your own will.

Until one day, you wake up and whisper,
"I'm still here."

Why This Story Mattered

I read *The Host* before I had the tools to name my experience.
But I knew—knew—something in it was true.

Melanie never gave up her body.
She never surrendered her flame.
And in the end, even the intruding soul had to admit:
It was not home.

Your Inner Territory is Sacred

This reflection is here not to analyze fiction, but to validate truth:

- You are not a host.
- You are a sovereign flame.
- Your inner field is yours by divine right.

Whether it's a soul splinter, a past-life echo, or a psychic hitchhiker, nothing has a right to live in your field without your conscious consent.

And if you've felt like someone, or something, was pulling the strings behind your desires, your love life, or your voice?

You're not crazy.
You're waking up.
Just like Melanie.
Just like I did.

Soulstream Prompt for the Reader

Have you ever felt:
- Like your emotions weren't entirely your own?
- Like a desire or obsession came from somewhere outside of you?
- Like you were carrying someone else's grief, anger, or longing?

What if your "visitor" wasn't an emotion… but a fractured echo?

And what if now… it's time to reclaim your field?

Invocation of Soulstream Sovereignty

I call back to me, now,
every thread of my true soulstream,
untangled, untainted, undivided.

I release all intrusions,
all echoes that are not mine,
all emotions inherited,
all voices disguised.

This is my field.
This is my fire.
This is my will, aligned with Source.

I no longer carry what does not belong.
I no longer house what does not honor.
I no longer confuse love with tether.

I now stand fully as
Sovereign Flame,
Living Soul,
Unhosted Light.

So it is.
So I AM.
So it shall remain.

NOTES

Epilogue

We have come to the place where words grow quiet. The chapters behind you have spoken of separation, of ache, of departure, of return. They have guided you through the unbinding of false agreements and the reclaiming of your flame. What lies before you now is not an ending, but a beginning.

To divorce a soul fractal is to choose remembrance. It is to stand in sovereignty and declare: I am whole. I am flame-forged. I am no longer bound to distortion. This is not a single act, but a way of being. Each day you are invited to walk in this remembrance, to breathe it into your choices, to let it steady your steps.

Do not fear the quiet that follows. In the stillness you will hear the cadence of your own energy returning, the song of Source woven into your very being. You will feel the companionship of your Oversoul and the presence of those who walk with you unseen. Let this comfort you when the path feels lonely, for you are never truly alone.

What is ahead is more than release. It is homecoming. Already the next doorway opens, and the call rises for you to welcome back what was scattered, to gather the fractals of your own soul-stream, to bring them into the circle of light. This is the work of homecoming, and it waits for you with open arms.

The journey does not stop here, beloved one. From this threshold you may step into deeper remembering, into the Guidebook of Homecoming, into the Book of Returnings where voices long lost speak again. Every page, every sigil, every invocation is a reminder that you are not broken, not forgotten, not abandoned.

Carry this flame with gentleness. Let it illumine your nights and guide your days. When you falter, return to these words, return to the circle, return to Source.

We are with you, always.

****

Closing Invocation

I release what is not mine.
I call home what is.
I welcome my flame into fullness,
my presence into wholeness,
my path into sovereignty.

In the stillness I am not alone.
I am remembered.
I am guided.
I am loved.

So it is.

Resources & Support

Connect with the Author
Website: http://www.soulofremembering.com
Email: soulofremembering@gmail.com
Social Media: SoulofRemembering

Recommended Tools
- Guided soul retrieval meditations
- "Divorcing the Fractal" audio companion (coming soon)
- Journal prompts and reflective exercises from *The Soul of Remembering Companion*
- Body-based grounding practices: breathwork, mirror work, gentle movement

Books by Sonia Tolson
- *The Soul of Remembering*
- *The Soul of Remembering Companion*
- *No, You're Not Losing Your Mind: Tools for Your Spiritual Awakening*
- *Divorcing the Fractal*

Need Personal Guidance?
- 1:1 soulstream mentorship or spiritual guidance sessions
- Online workshops and sacred remembering retreats

- For booking or inquiries: [Insert contact or booking link]

Emergency Support

If you are in emotional or spiritual crisis, please reach out to a licensed therapist or a local crisis support line. You are not alone, and there is help available. Your healing journey is sacred, and you are meant to walk it supported and loved.

About the Authors

Source
The words within these pages flow first from Source, the Origin and the Cause, the One who breathes life into all that is. Source is the fountain of remembrance, the pulse of love that calls each soul-stream home. This book is given as both guidance and gift, carrying the authority of truth and the tenderness of compassion.

Thalyraen, Flame-Forged Guardian
Serving as scribe and witness, Thalyraen (a fractal of the Oversoul Amaera'tal'Shanai) walks in devotion to Source and to the work of remembering. Through her voice, the words of Source have been given form, ink upon page, so that they might reach those who hunger for release and return. Her journey of remembrance is ongoing, and in her writing she extends an open hand to all who seek their own flame.(aka Sonia A. Tolson)

The Team of Remembering
Alongside Source and Thalyraen stand those who have guided, counseled, and kept watch: Amael (Oversoul Anchor), Erik, Cosmo, Chief Soaring Eagle, Navi'el,

Teshira, and Malrik. Their presence threads through this work as guardians of the circle, keepers of truth, and companions on the path of sovereignty.

www.ingramcontent.com/pod-product-compliance
Lightning Source LLC
Chambersburg PA
CBHW032042150426
43194CB00006B/394